# GETTING YOUR TEENAGER THROUGH THEIR EXAMS

*Practical, down to earth advice on revision and exams for parents and carers.*

Lee Jackson

## Dedication:

To Clare, Rhea and Lauren for their patience and laughs as I researched and wrote this.

# ABOUT THE AUTHOR

Lee Jackson has written many books for adults and teenagers including "How to Enjoy And Succeed at School and College" and is one of the most experienced and popular motivational school speakers in the UK.

He has worked in schools for over 23 years and works in every type of UK school and college.His website is www.LeeJackson.biz His twitter account is @leejackson

# CONTENTS

# INTRODUCTION

Dear Parent or Carer,

The timing of this booklet for me couldn't have been more ironic.

I'm the author of many books. Three of them have been about teenagers, two about how to help them do well and pass exams in schools.

I've helped teenage students for years, as a youth worker and for the last eight years as a motivational speaker working in schools up and down the UK.

What makes the timing of writing this booklet so perfect and ironic, is that right now my 16 year old identical twin girls are in the middle of their final GCSE exams.

Yup, no more theories for me, no more let me speak from my ivory tower 'professional experience'. This is real. Right now, I'm the Dad of GCSE taking twins. A Dad who is supposed to be an "expert" in motivating teenagers for success! No more dress rehearsals. I'm going to find out if "my stuff" actually works for my teens! Gulp.

I want this booklet to be helpful, down-to-earth and ultimately an encouragement for you as you guide your teenagers through the last years of their school career. I want to be honest and 'real world' - that's who I am, and I think it's the only way we can survive this challenging time as parents. Please forgive the lack of deep and complex educational theories, I don't think this is the place for them. This is designed to be practical and based on real life parenting not 'Hollywood" parenting, if you know what I mean.

The main thing I hope for you though, is that you learn that you're not alone, and the challenges that you and your child face are quite normal Many others before you have found their way through in one piece.

Parenting is complex. We rarely get trained for it and sadly it can be very lonely too. For the sixteen years I've been a Dad, my wife Clare and I have wondered whether or not we are doing the right thing, whether stuff that happens is 'normal', and to be honest we've often just had to muddle through and try things out, working it all out as we go along. All I can offer is my honesty, research and my real life experience, I hope it helps.

*Parenting expert Rob Parsons says that being a parent is like being on a river in a small boat. Sometimes it's calm and sunny, other times we simply hit the rapids. They don't last forever, the calm will return eventually, but the rapids are real and make us hold on tight.*

This short book covers two main things: Parenting skills to help you, and study skills that you can understand and suggest to help your child.

…Because that's the ultimate combination to help your child get through this key time. We as parents do our bit and they do their bit.

The underlying principle of the research I've done and the talks I do in schools/colleges is simply this: 98% of us have to go to school so we may as well make the best of it.

It's as simple as that, let's not waste our time doing re-sits at College but focus now and get the best out of school.

Very few people truly enjoy(ed) school, but we can all make the most of it, with some help along the way.

# PARENTING SKILLS

I remember former Prime Minister Tony Blair started to get into hot water because he started talking quite seriously about parenting skills. it's a tricky subject, and it's literally too close to home. The fact remains, we don't get trained for this and we are all in different places. We all have both good and bad parenting experiences in our past, all of which make up our view and our day-to-day practice of parenting. In fact only today I saw a parent shouting at their child in the super market as people looked on judgementally. In my opinion as human beings our most difficult job is to bring up another human being. Well done for getting this far!

Here are a few skills that I've learned both as a professional working in schools and as a Dad of teenagers, and before you think I'm some kind of Super dad I'm not. I've failed many times just like everyone else, but these things I've found have helped:

# BE A 'COACH' NOT JUST A 'MANAGER'

I really believe in changing our view of parenting into becoming our child's 'coach' not just their 'manager'. People who manage tend to manage 'stuff' not people and, like me, you've probably been on the wrong end of a bad manager at some point in your working life. They can be negative, jobsworth and not much fun to be around but a coach is a different thing altogether.

Coaching our teens gets the best out of them. We become an encourager not just a nagging voice. In the world of sport coaches are everywhere, they help the teams and athletes be the best they're capable of being. A good coach will of course have to tell you off when you're not doing so well but really their job is to encourage and to keep you on track so you can do more than you think you are capable of doing.

My friend Matt is a top-flight basketball coach I've seen him win games and lose games but what I see most in him is the ability to steer, adjust and encourage his players to get through, overcome, and even enjoy the tough games that they have to play. Even when players are taken off the court they're not shouted at but given a reassuring hi-five. They don't get a lecture because in

10 minutes time they may have to go on again. I think that parenting is always about choosing the right battle at the right time, because there are many battles and we can't fight them all. Exam time particularly is the key time to let some things slide and to focus on what's important - getting them through their exams in the right frame of mind with full support from us and our families. Exams are a just a season they don't last forever (thankfully!) and they just require focus from everyone.

# COACHING PHRASES TO USE WHEN TALKING TO YOUR TEEN:

"How do you feel today?"

"How do you feel your revision is going?"

"What do you need from me at the moment?"

"You'll be fine, you'll make it, we've just got to get through this time together."

"It won't be long now, just get your head down for a bit and keep on going - you'll make it."

"Remember afterwards you'll enjoy maybe one of the longest holidays in your life!"

# BE POSITIVE WITH OUR CHILDREN

I don't like to tell people to 'be positive' as it almost seems aggressive to me. But the fact remains that a positive attitude from us as parents makes a real difference to our children's success in school.

I like to think of being *'realistically positive'.*

What we need to be doing:

- Finding out where they are with their estimated grades (teachers/reports can tell you this)

-  helping them to believe the positive truth about themselves (i.e that they can do well, and certainly better than they probably believe)

- Being positive towards their exams and their f uture.

- Being positive towards learning and the school.

Often in my talks in mainstream schools I ask the students "do you realise that you are here for a reason? You're here because you can make it, you can do it, otherwise, to be frank, you wouldn't be in this school, you'd be somewhere else". Sometimes I can see the light go on in their heads at this point, and I often see a "Yeah, he's right" smile start to develop as their confidence grows. It's great to see that. It's one of the reasons I do what I do. The occasional 'lightbulb' moment, keeps me going.

# WHAT MY CAR TAUGHT ME ABOUT MY TEENAGERS TAKING EXAMS

I got a nearly new car a couple of years ago, it was great, but after a few weeks a strange noise started. It was a weird noise - a kind of a scraping. I listened for a few days and noticed it only real happened when I went around corners at speed. I thought there was an issue with the rear suspension, it didn't sound good at all. It was definitely coming from the back of the car. I was just about the ring the garage and book it in for a full check up when I thought I'd just have a look around. I opened the boot and sat in, bouncing the car, moving the car trying to get it to repeat the noise. I grabbed the seats and the trim, punching, moving and checking anything I could. And then I saw it! In the back of the car are two extra seats that flip up when we need them, and next to these rarely used seats are cup holders, and in the left hand cup holder was a 2p piece. This 2p piece stayed still until I went around a corner at speed and then it moved in the holder making a scraping noise above the rear suspension! I'd found it! Finding this little 2p piece saved me time, effort and money. I'm so glad I found it and yes, I felt both smug and stupid at the same time - if that's possible. It wasn't the suspension falling apart after all! Phew.

We all know our teens well, we are the experts, well at least we were until they become teens taking exams, and then it got trickier. But before we jump off at the deep end thinking they have this big issue or that big issue, we need to just check the little things. I learned this  the hard way with that 2p piece. How do they feel about school? How are they getting on with their friends? Have they got the right revision/exam kit? How are they feeling about the exams coming up? Have they done a revision plan? Just keeping an eye on them, feeding them and encouraging them maybe all they need to get through their exams. Any other ongoing teenage issues we have parental  concern about we can probably deal with later, but for now check for the 2p piece and get through this season as painlessly as you can. This might help...

# BE POSITIVE IN OUR DEALINGS WITH THE SCHOOL

Schools and teachers aren't perfect, but I really do believe 99% of them try their best. They will fail us from time to time but unless there's a very serious issue, we need to try and work **with** the school not against the school. Schools have so much data on the academic progress of GCSE students these days that they can track progress on a weekly basis, this is exhausting for teachers but really useful as parents. My teens' school use a traffic light system on half termly reports so even at a glance we can see. Green's for good, amber for needs attention and red for needs serious attention. It's helpful to know where they are at. If you ever have any questions about progress I'm sure your school would be happy to chat to you. Many have non-teaching heads of years now who have more time for meeting parents too. I even have the mobile number of my teens' head of year, but most schools won't offer that service.

# THE BIG FEAR

As I study people, the 'self-help' industry and motivation there are two things that come up time and time again. Self esteem and the fear of failure. Self esteem is the lens we look through as we see the world and our relationships and that often can be affected by the fear of failure. We all suffer from it in one sense or another. Can you remember a time or event where the fear of failure has taken over? I teach presentation skills a lot and it's often the biggest fear in that context, and it can last for a lifetime. Your child maybe suffering from it too. If they are reluctant to start revising or to work hard, it's often, but not always, rooted in the fear of failure. When I'm working in a challenging school I see this a lot. The students can almost persuade themselves that if they do no work at all then when they fail it'll be somehow easier on them. But if they really put the effort in and then still 'don't make the grade' it'll be a disaster for them. So they figure out that not trying is less embarrassing. It's scary being a 15/16 year old! We can help our teens with this by letting them know that as Zig Ziglar once said "Failure is an event not a person." I fail, you've failed, we all have. In fact I spoke at an event last year all about failure. I even collect stories of people who've failed, but most of

those stories finish with the time they picked
themselves back up again.

Failure is part of life. It's a learning point for our
children's future. We all may fail, but we need to learn
to have the grit to get back up again. GCSEs can teach
them that. If they give them their best shot, they often
get better results than they thought they would. That's
because working hard is a life changer.

# I CAN'T / I WON'T

Often when people say "I can't" do something they really mean "I won't" do that and the fear of failure kicks in again. The trick as a parent exam coach(!) is to realise this and encourage them that they can do it - bit by bit, step by step. Shouting at them won't work, but little encouragements will. More carrot, less stick works with students who are frozen by past failures.

# REWARDS AND INCENTIVES

Rewards can work really well to help keep motivated. Some teens respond to small financial rewards, treats or clothes etc, but many don't. Find out the 'little trophies' and the 'big trophies' that work for you, what you can use as a treat and reward for hard work not just great results. It's more about rewarding effort, if your child is putting in the effort then reward them daily with comments and the occasional treat. Then maybe talk about a 'big trophy' (reward) at the end. Some parents offer big financial rewards as an incentive, this might work for some, but can have downsides too. We've tried to take a different approach. One of my daughters has been invited to go on a cheap foreign holiday with a friend (and their grandparents) after her exams and so that's become her focus, and we have encouraged and rewarded her towards that. We haven't paid for it but we've paid bits of it and helped her to get ready for it. As you know spending time **with** your teens while doing stuff that they want to do is often better than just giving them money. Coffee shop / bagel house trips seem to work well in the Jackson house. Be creative and reward effort in your own family style. We all need a carrot occasionally.

# PENS AND PENCILS

One nice way to signal this important season is to check that they have got all the school equipment they need. Do they have good blue/black/coloured pens, pencils, the right calculator for maths (we've lost two!) and any other good stuff. If they like stationery it's a great chance to treat them if they don't have the right things - it helps them to know that it's time to get serious about the studies and having the right equipment is a key to that . Even now when I go to speak to a year group of Y11's often only weeks or days before their exams many still don't have a pen with them. Cheap but branded, not generic pens are most reliable I reckon.

# THE BUS STOP THEORY

I once heard persuasion expert Shelle Rose Charvet talk about bus stops. This short talk helped the penny to drop for me when talking to teens, I teach the theory often when training teachers and youth workers.

She wasn't talking about real world bus stops but personal bus stops. We all have a bus stop, we stand at our own bus stop. We stand there and wait. We often see others at their bus stops too, including our teens. We wave at them, but we often just stay at our bus stop. As human beings when we want to talk to someone - we call to them from our bus stop and tell them to come to see us. Sometimes we even have to shout to get their attention, we shout to get them to move to our bus stop. Our bus stop is nice, it's comfortable, it has our own rules, the buses run on time and it suits us just fine. But I've learnt as a youth worker, speaker and Dad that to really talk to young people, we have to move from the comfort of our bus stop and move towards theirs. This act of moving closer to them, of seeing life from their bus stop breaks down barriers, opens up conversations and reduces confrontation.

So, in the real world what does this look like? It can be as simple as this - instead of sitting on the sofa telling our teens to come and talk to us about school, exams or life we simply get up, knock on their bedroom door, after the mumbled "yeah", pop our head around the door and chat, using open questions and body language (open questions are like the coaching questions I mentioned earlier, not questions that can be answered in a simple yes or no). The holy grail is when we get to perch on the end of their bed (keeping on their level or lower is a good move here rather than towering over them with our arms folded potentially looking intimidating) and just have an open chat. If the bedroom isn't a good option I often find that the car works just as well, especially with lads, as there's something about a drive where we don't stare each other in the eye that encourages good conversation. My wife Clare and I

have had some great talks with my teens when perched on the ends of their beds or driving them somewhere. It doesn't always work but it's a great start.

The other things that I think work really well too are saying sorry when we've messed up or been grumpy with them, and also making sure they are alone when we chat and their siblings aren't there chipping in every ten-seconds - a scene I'm sure you're all very familiar with! Don't get me wrong I still banter with my teens, but using the bus stop technique works really well and as long as we can say sorry and laugh occasionally too, it's a great tool for our parenting toolbox. Make it work for you in your home, you could even cheekily try it at work too. Experiment with it.

# WORK HARD

They've been told it a thousand times by teachers and by you – that's because it's true - hard work (esp. smart work) works! It gets us from where we are to where we want to be and is much more reliable than a lottery or an X-Factor audition!

Controversial American author Larry Winget has written a book called "It's called work for a reason" and while I often cringe at his blunt, brash style he has a point. If we are lucky enough to have a job that we enjoy then that's amazing. I love my job, but that still doesn't mean it's easy. Sitting here at my computer writing this doesn't magically happen, I've had to lock myself way and get it done. I love communicating with good people like yourself but I don't enjoy being stuck on a computer typing when I could be out in the sunshine. But today I am. It's called work for a reason. The trick with teens though is to tell them this without sounding like a song on repeat (we used say 'like a broken record!'). Show them how hard work has worked for you and encourage them to keep on going like you've had to learn yourself.

GCSEs or A-levels is a season of hard work, it doesn't last forever, and as one headteacher said to me the other day "Lee, at the end of the day I get 13 weeks of holiday a year, I try not to forget that." A school year is about 37 weeks, so encourage them to work when they have to and enjoy the breaks when they come.

# SLEEP

In recent studies teenagers and their sleeping patterns have been looked into. There's no doubt that their bodies and minds are in growth mode and need sleep to help that, but also good studying needs sleep too. Check your child's bedroom. Is their bed comfortable? Do they have blackout curtains? But most of all what pre-sleep routine do they have? Getting them into a good routine sets them up for good results and for the rest of their life. Late night food binging, distractions, arguments and too much screen time before bed can cause sleeplessness. So encourage them to eat well, and get ready for bed at a reasonable time with the right routine. Which brings me onto the parenting hot potato…

# MOBILE PHONES, SCREENS AND TABLETS!

In some recent press article "teenagers" have been re-named "screenagers".

According to the Kaiser Family Foundation  the average 8-18 year old spends 7 hours and 38 minutes using media (i.e. in front of screen) on a daily basis. That's over 53 hours a week.

When I speak to parents that I know or when doing parents evenings - this is their biggest battle or "flashpoint" these days. It's a tricky subject, but there is hope, according to the Kaiser study - 'Only about three in ten young people say they have rules about how much time they can spend watching TV (28%) or playing video games (30%), and 36% say the same about using the computer.  But when parents *do* set limits, children spend less time with media. Those with *any* media rules consume nearly 3 hours less media per day (2:52) than those with no rules.' It's up to us, during the GCSE or A-level  courses, and especially as the final few months approach, there simply aren't enough hours in the day for teens to consume that amount of media and do well in their revision/exams. It just can't be done.

I think the best way is to make some good family wide rules, slowly and steadily. Maybe decide to all leave your phones downstairs at night for example. We love a bit of TV but our teens don't have one in their bedroom and they don't have a computer either. They have a smartphone of course like many do, but we negotiate about that a lot and their phone is always the first thing to go when we feel the need for sanctions. Removing a phone or just a wifi code may be the most powerful thing we have in our parental tool bag. Most teens have phones and are on social media - but they can affect their concentration levels, studies and revision skills...

[1] *http://kff.org/disparities-policy/press-release/daily-media-use-among-children-and-teens-up-dramatically-from-five-years-ago/*

# THE POWER OF FOCUS

Remember those old camcorders with the big red button on the back of the handle? Well, it turns out that our brain loves a record button. According to a 2015 Penn State study  our brain needs us to press the 'record' button to work properly.

It seems like memory is like a camcorder. If you don't hit the 'record' button on the camcorder, it's not going to 'remember' what the lens is pointed at. But if you do hit the 'record' button - in this case, you know what you're going to be asked to remember -- then the information is stored." Sometimes, our teens all like to think that they just take stuff in and retain it without trying, but that just isn't the case. To really use our memory well and for us to help our teens to retain the information they need for exams we must help them to learn to press that record button.

But how?

## FOCUS

Purely focusing on a piece of work or revision will make a big difference. Even just encouraging our children to switch off all distractions for an hour or so can mean the difference between getting the grade they deserve or not.

Our phone and social media **can** be switched off.

When I go into schools, I joke about the *'off'* button being the same button as the 'on' button - I say it as a joke, but I've met people who genuinely never switch off their phone, ever. They are the people who keep twitching every time they hear an electronic bleep and don't sleep at night without checking their instagram 'likes'. Scary. If we help our children focus and reduce their distractions in a quiet room ready for work. I'll guarantee them two things:

1. They'll get on better with their work

2. When they do switch on their phone again they will still have friends! Trust me on this. It may sound very radical to them but it is worth it and more importantly it does work.

Don't panic, I reckon we'd all survive if we switched off our phones once in a while.

[2]*'Seeing is not remembering'... Wyble/Chen, Penn State, Jan. 2015:*
*http://news.psu.edu/story/341711/2015/01/21/research/seeing-not-remembering*

# LISTENING TO MUSIC WHILE STUDYING, DOES IT HELP OR HINDER?

Even listening to music has been proven to distract us when doing work. Dr Nick Perham from the University of Wales Institute did a study in 2010 with students and discovered that listening to music while trying to revise lessened the ability for us to recall the information. So, if they are serious about doing well – talk about switching off their music for a bit too - peace and quiet will make them more creative and smarter when working. But don't worry he also says listening to their favourite music before working helps too. So let them play music loud before and after – just not **during** their work. I just heard 'Sweet Child of Mine' by Guns & Roses on the radio today and cranked it right up, just before I wrote this, in peace and quiet!

I often listen to music while working but always instrumental music not music with lyrics. Words distract. Spotify and other online music services have instrumental/study playlists ready and waiting for students who hate absolute silence now.

Good work is sometimes just about focusing on the right thing at the right time.

"

*Concentrate all your thoughts upon the work at hand. The sun's rays do not burn until brought to a focus.*

"

*- Alexander Graham Bell (Inventor of the telephone 1847-1922)*

# GROUP STUDY

Group study can be a great thing to break up the monotony and loneliness of revision, but like anything else it can be a reason for procrastination too. It can work well for modern foreign languages but not so well for more technical subjects. If they want to do group study, then fantastic but it needs to have a goal or purpose or it can be a big time waster. Ask what they are going to study and encourage them, but be aware that it can be a reason to not do work. I know that from my own revision experience from when I was 16!

# THE OLYMPIC LEGACY

In 2012 during the London Olympics a new phrase entered our vocabulary - 'Marginal gains'. Marginal gains as described by British Cycling's performance director Dave Brailsford is finding out all the factors that go into riding a bike faster and increasing them by 1% to see much better performance. He even talked about learning to wash their hands properly so they didn't get ill as often and taking the same pillow to sleep on to feel better. All the little things add up, and marginal gains can take our children from where they are to where they want to be. From a 'D' to a 'B' for example. It won't happen overnight, but bit by bit, day by day it will add up and their results will change. We just have to help them make the changes that make the difference. Better results won't happen without changing the little things that affect the overall picture. We have to change and keep on going to see the results we want.

It can be done.

# SO, WHAT OVERALL REVISION TECHNIQUE IS PROVEN TO WORK WHEN GETTING READY FOR GCSE EXAMS?

In my Collins study skills book I talk about the gift of time. We all have it, we can all use it well if we choose. No matter who we are in life: 'important' 'vip' 'famous' 'rich' or just 'normal', we all have the same amount of time in the day (86,400 seconds to be precise). One of the keys to good revision and study skills is to use time well and to start early. It's proven to work. In fact in 2013 Prof John Dunlovsky the co-author of the snappily titled "Improving Students' Learning With Effective Learning Techniques: Promising Directions From Cognitive and Educational Psychology report"(!) mentions 'distributed practice' as the best technique,(to you and me that's starting early and revising regularly). He says it is the "most powerful" of all the strategies.

Simple and effective.

# STAND UP AND STICK UP

When people talk about studying and revision I always find it odd that people presume that you can only sit down! We do have to sit for some things but often with me when I sit down my brain checks out!

Being active when studying is so key. Even fitness apps on SmartWatches now tell us every now and again to stand up and walk, we've become too inactive in our daily lives. When your child is using post-it notes or cards they can be written standing up, and then they can be stuck up on the walls of their bedroom too. Getting key facts onto walls is a great way to remember stuff they need as the course progresses. In all the work I've done with teenage lads I think this is particularly important for them, as they have a rise in their testosterone levels mid-morning too, which makes them restless. If they get restless they can stand up and walk around. I often do this when I'm in big meetings or conferences, as I'd rather stand up and walk around at the back taking in information than be slumped in my seat half asleep or on social media like most audiences are.

# PROCRASTINATION…

…is probably the longest word I know and one of the most seductive. Some people have put the pro in procrastination - including myself at times! When exams are approaching it's weird how Cash In The Attic, Bargain Hunt, and other daytime TV programmes become so attractive.

The other word for procrastination is Facebook! Have a chat about procrastination and work on a few strategies to stop its effects.

**Here are a few simple suggestions:**

Get the ball rolling, starting is tough so do something that gets you going.

Once you are going, start the big fat horrible task **first**.

Start by chipping away at it, much like I've done with this booklet, I've done it in steps and chunks, I haven't sat and done the whole thing in one sitting - that would have over-awed and ultimately, frozen me.

Reward yourself once you've done something big, a chocolate bar with a tea break after you've done a big task can be a powerful (and more tasty) carrot.

Tell someone to ask you if you've done it - accountability can be a powerful tool.

Remember perfectionism is the fuel for procrastination - it's much better to start imperfect than to sit there just thinking about something being perfect.

Doing nothing isn't 'doing nothing', it's a choice that we make.

# MIND MAPS®[3]

Mind maps are a skill to learn, and can be a real help depending on the personality type of the student. I find that simple 'spider graphs' work well for me - I don't need to use fifteen different coloured felt tips and little diagrams to get my brain working and remembering. Just a blank page and some lines and text help me but your child might enjoy and use full colour mind maps - I'm sure their school can help them here if not Google for quick tutorials on mind maps, Youtube is full of them.

[3] Mind Map® and Mind Maps® are registered trademarks of The Buzan Organisation

# WHO'S ON THEIR TEAM?

If you could write down the team that will get your child the grades they deserve, who'd be on it? Yourself, your partner, teachers, youth workers, mentors, tutors, family members, family friends, friendly listening ears?

Make sure that these people know the season that your child is in as they may be able to offer a friendly meeting, phone call, text or coffee shop trip to help to see them through. Even if you are a single parent, you don't have to do this all on your own.

Who's on their team? Get recruiting.

# HOME ENVIRONMENT

Our home is, just that, our home. There's no place like it and it should be our favourite place to be. For teenagers taking GCSEs or A-levels home becomes very important and their own space is a special place, no matter how grumpy they appear.

Maybe the best thing we can do as parents is to establish their roots as they grow their wings. All parenting books talk about the roots and wings concept. As they grow up and become more responsible and independent (at various rates of success!) the home is key. So we can help them at school by helping them be at home in a comfortable way while knowing in the back of our minds that we are helping them to grow wings now and learn to fly in the 'big world' out there. Exams are part of that process, they are being tested externally now on their performance - something that becomes part of everyday working life. As we help them prepare for their final exams we are helping them get ready for the life ahead of them, a life that we won't feature in quite so much.

That's part of this process, as painful as it may seem, it's the truth, prepare them well now and you have done your main job well.

# LEARNING FROM LOWRY

One of the big lessons for me in life is that learning lasts a lifetime. I've learned so much now in my mid-40's. More than I learned in school to be honest, I love it, even though I'm not a 'natural book person' I still learn in many ways. School can be stressful, but if we can, let's use school as a launchpad for lifelong learning. If we can get them through this and they still like to learn we can tell ourselves it's a job well done.

My favourite painter is L.S. Lowry famous for his matchstick figures of industrial Britain, I recently found out that until the day he died he still took painting lessons.

I love that.

# THE WOBBLES

A very tall building will wobble to allow it to stay upright in the wind or during earthquakes. We all have our wobbles too. Exams can be stressful and we need to look out for real signs of stress, but also have in mind that they will wobble. That's all part of the process. The occasional wobble is ok, hold on tight. Ask other parents about the wobbles their teens have had, you will get through it.

No storm lasts forever.

# FILMS AND THEATRE TRIPS

Often trips can help their revision too. My teens were studying the book 'To Kill A Mocking Bird' and we found out that it was on at the local theatre. I haven't seen a play in years but we all went - it was a good night out and they picked up other stuff that they can use when in the exam. They loved us being part of their studies. We were lucky there, but many books they are studying have been made into films - get the dvd and watch it together. Maybe even a trip to a museum might help too.

# REVISION PLAN

A good revision plan is a must - you can make your own (don't take too long on it though!) or you can download one for free from Collins here:

http://is.gd/freerevisionplanner

# REST AND RELAXATION...

...is a good habit to encourage. It may not seem probable but is possible for teens to over work for exams. During the busy pre-exam season especially, just staring at books for hours isn't being productive. In the last few weeks, just weeks from their GCSEs my twin daughters have been watching TV, seeing friends, going to youth group and doing fitness classes too, it's good to encourage exercise and breaks as much as work.

The two feed each other.

In fact I'm just writing this section after spending an hour having a coffee with my wife. I needed a break, and now I'm being more productive again.

Can you encourage them to timetable fun/rest/exercise onto their revision/exam timetable too?

# GETTING AND USING EXTRA HELP

If you feel that your child needs further help then you have a few options. The first one is to ask the school. There will most likely be after school classes, holiday revision, as well as past papers online on the learning platform that the school uses.

We told our teens that from Christmas in Y11 the school day would finish later as they should go to all extra classes on offer - it's only another hour a day and has been really helpful to them. You can, of course, choose to pay for extra tutoring as well, which may be an option for a certain subject.

# THE TEENAGE SCALE OF STUDY!

Where is your child on this scale when it comes to study and revision?

Laid back/horizontal <————> Keen/worrier

Teens react in different ways to school. Some can almost over study and be stressed out, while others virtually don't realise that they are in their exam years! Once you know where they are at, you can learn the strategies to help them succeed.

There's no right or wrong it's just different personality types and backgrounds.

Even we as parents can be on our own scale too when it comes to the pressure we put on our children.

Where are you on the nag scale?

Again, it's not right or wrong it's just who we are, that said, we, as well as our children will need to make some adjustments in the exam years. As I've mentioned before we can't fight every battle, but we must establish boundaries around their time and school work, otherwise the work of the school will be wasted, without our support.

Never mention study <———> Always nagging them

# WHAT DO OTHER PARENTS THINK WORKS BEST?

**I asked a few and have summarised the responses here:**

*What do you think is the BIGGEST thing a parent or carer can do to help their children through their GCSEs?*

• Stay calm and be supportive, not pressuring.

• Be actively involved with school. Keep in touch with class teachers, regularly read and respond to comments in the planner, make yourself aware of what's going on.

• Encourage them to do their best and that their best is good enough.

• Tell them you are proud of them and that you love them.

• Get the fridge and cupboards stocked with nice treats and snacks for the duration of the exams.

- Make sure home is calm, warm, and that there is no tension. Make sure the journey to school is stress free too if possible.

- Recognise how stressful this time is for teens. Strike bargains - build in ice cream and video nights.

- They appear to not want to be with parents but they need to.

- Create a peaceful place for the children to study. Be interested in the subjects they are revising.

- The bomb site / dumping ground - which is the offspring's bedroom will not be commented on for the duration of the exams.

Many thanks to Andrea, Helen, Andy, Rob and others for their answers.

# AS THE MAIN EXAMS DRAW NEAR...

The amount of revision and work to do will seem overwhelming to your child. This is where prioritisation becomes the key to exam success:

Get them to find out the key things to revise and prioritise those. Then get them to do the hard stuff first - maybe the subjects they don't like to work on are actually the most important. Get the teachers help to prioritise, and do a plan so that they don't feel swamped by the amount they have to do. And once again just remind them that it's only for a season.

# REVISION - IN A NUTSHELL FOR BUSY TEENAGERS

- Find out **when** the exam is

- Find out **what** you **have** to revise for it

- Make a quick revision plan (don't spend more than 30 mins doing this!)

- **Start** revising…

- Start early, don't just cram the night before, spread out the subjects

- Read your books/notes, then make your own revision cards/post-its /mind-maps

- Take breaks and reward yourself

- Test yourself or get others to test you

- Do past papers in timed exam conditions

- Ask for help / feedback from teachers

- Switch off your phone so you can focus

- Prioritise the key topics as the exam moves closer

- Prepare your brain and body the night before an exam with good food and a good night's rest, then glance over your notes before the exam in the morning

- Take the exam

- Reward yourself knowing you've given it your best shot

- Enjoy the results you get

- Smile smugly and enjoy your long holiday :)

# QUICK-FIRE TIPS - IN NO PARTICULAR ORDER....

- Help your child understand the big reason for doing their studies. If they know the BIG reason It can be very motivating and can help to create good habits. E.g. You are doing exams to help you get to the career you want or the University or College course that you want to do. You are doing maths to help you in later life when you will need to use it in everyday tasks like business accounts, online banking, and balancing cash registers (all things I've had to do in the workplace. Have you?)

- Encourage them not to use lined paper but use plain paper - its helps as they can use it to do mind-mapping and 'spider-graphs.' etc.

- Find out what works best for them - what keeps them motivated and engaged? Try different strategies. You'll find a combination that works.

- They can read their text books and notes and make them into audio files on their phones, then when you are travelling or away from a desk/home they can use them to remind themselves about facts and use the info to revise.

- Encourage them to talk to their positive friends, the friends that'll keep them going and on task. A good positive chat is so helpful.

- Revision, rest and recreation all go together.

- Fifteen minutes focused study followed by a five minute break is better than 1 hour staring into space. Find the best timings to suit their brains. Use kitchen timers or countdown apps to time their study times.

- The best revision is the revision that was started weeks or months ago, the next best is the one that is started now.

- We all have 86,400 seconds a day, no matter who we are, It's all about how we use that time in the run up to exams.

- "Working hard is important but there is something that matters even more: believing in yourself" Harry Potter - spoken in the film "The Order of The Phoenix"

- There are lots of short, snappy and helpful videos for students on my Youtube channel: https://www.youtube.com/user/leejacksonspeaker

- Please send me your tips too you can find me at http://leejackson.biz

John Erskine (1879-1951) was a Professor at Colombia University in the United States. He was known as an educator, pianist, the author of 60 books and a witty lecturer. He famously said:

"

*Let's tell young people the best books are yet to be written; the best painting, the best government the best of everything is yet to be done by them.*

"

I agree.

I wish you and your child every success.